Leaping Learners
Education, LLC

For more information and resources visit us at:
www.leapinglearnersed.com

©Sean Bulger

Published by Leaping Learners, LLC, Verona, NJ 07044 . All rights reserved. Reproduction in whole or inpart without written permission of the publisher is prohibited.

Every attempt has been made to credit each photo. Please contact us if there has been an error and we will resolve the issue.

All design by Sean Bulger
All other pictures by Sean Bulger or royalty free from Pixabay.com

ISBN
978-1-948569-12-5

Dear Parents and Guardians,

Thank you for purchasing a *Clayton Teaches About* series book! After teaching students from kindergarten to second grade for more than seven years, I became frustrated by the lack of engaging books my students could read independently. To help my students engage with nonfiction topics, my wife and I decided to write nonfiction books for children. We hope to inspire young children to learn about the natural world.

Here at Leaping Learners Education, LLC, we have three main goals:

1. Spark young readers' curiosity about the natural world
2. Develop critical independent reading skills at an early age
3. Develop reading comprehension skills before and after reading

We hope your child enjoys learning with Clayton. If you or your children are interested in a topic we have not written about yet, send us an email with your topic, and maybe your book will be next!

                                        Thank you,

                                      Sean Bulger, Ed.M

www.leapinglearnersed.com

Reading Suggestions:

Before reading this book, encourage your children to do a "picture walk" where they skim through the book looking the pictures to help them think about what they already know about the topic. Thinking back about what they already know helps children to get excited about learning more facts and begin reading with some confidence.

Preview any new vocabulary words with your child. Have your child use the phrase in their own words to see if they understand the definition.

After previewing the book, encourage your child to read the book independently more than once. After they have finished reading, encourage them to complete the reading comprehension exercises at the end of the book to strengthen their reading skills!

This book is best for ages 5-6

but. . .
Please be mindful that reading levels are a guide and vary depending on a child's skills and needs.

Brown

Written by Sean Bulger

Hi! My name is Clayton. As you can see... I am a crayon! Come and learn about the color brown with me.

Some bears are **brown**. They live in the forest.

Some guitars are **brown**. People play music with them.

Some bagels are **brown**. People eat bagels for breakfast.

Some bags are **brown**. People use bags to carry things.

Pretzels are **brown**. Pretzels taste salty.

Some deer are **brown**. They eat plants and grass.

Wood is **brown**. Wood comes from trees.

Some dogs are **brown**. People have dogs as pets.

Do you know anything else that is brown? Draw it!

_____ is brown.

Do you know anything else that is brown? Draw it!

_____ is brown.

Find and circle the word "some"

am

some

they

some

same

The

they

We

am

The

we

some

same

Find and circle the word "people"

people

am

The   See

play

           you
See   We

See
     people   place

place   The
              am

people   you

www.ingramcontent.com/pod-product-compliance
Lightning Source LLC
Chambersburg PA
CBHW040025050426
42452CB00003B/137